The National Board Certification Workbook

The National Board Certification Workbook
How to Prepare Your Portfolio

Adrienne Mack-Kirschner

HEINEMANN
Portsmouth, NH

HEINEMANN
A division of Reed Elsevier Inc.
361 Hanover Street
Portsmouth, NH 03801–3912
www.heinemann.com

Offices and agents throughout the world

The author and the publisher wish to thank those who have generously given permission to reprint borrowed material:

Cover image of the National Board Certification box used courtesy of the National Board for Professional Teaching Standards.

Library of Congress Cataloging-in-Publication Data
Mack-Kirschner, Adrienne, 1944–
     The National Board certification workbook : how to prepare your portfolio /
Adrienne Mack-Kirschner.
        p. cm.
     Includes bibliographical references.
     ISBN 0-325-00564-8

     1. Teachers—Certification—United States—Handbooks, manuals, etc. 2. Education—
Standards—United States—Handbooks, manuals, etc. 3. National Board for Professional
Teaching Standards (U.S.)—Handbooks, manuals, etc. I. Title.
     LB1771 .M25 2003
     379.1′58—dc21   2002151326

Editor: Lois Bridges
Production coordinator: Elizabeth Valway
Production service: Lisa S. Garboski, bookworks
Cover design: Lisa Fowler
Composition: Argosy Publishing
Manufacturing: Steve Bernier

Printed in the United States of America on acid-free paper
07 06 05 04 03 ML 1 2 3 4 5

Contents

Introduction

Staff development is something that is done to you.
Professional development is something you do for yourself.

The National Board for Professional Teaching Standards is the highest and most comprehensive professional development experience you can give yourself. Although your initial goal may be to achieve certification on your first attempt, once you have completed the portfolio and the assessment center exercises you will agree with thousands of other teachers in saying that the professional growth you've experienced, the personal renewal, was its own reward.

Whether you are a candidate yourself, or a support provider for teacher-candidates, follow along the pages of this interactive workbook, which will guide you as you examine your teaching practices and prepare for National Board Certification.

The companion book, *The Teacher's Guide to National Board Certification: Unpacking the Standards*, will deepen candidates' knowledge about the core propositions underlying all of the certificate specific standards. While it is not mandatory to begin with the Guide before advancing to the Workbook, it is strongly recommended. The Guide can also serve as a valuable text for professional discussions around teaching and learning.

I love hearing from candidates and support providers. Each encounter allows me to deepen my own knowledge of the National Board process and to revise tools to benefit candidates.

Visit my website: *www.accomplishedteaching.com* or contact me directly via email: *nbpts@sbcglobal.net.*

The journey is the destination.

NUTS AND BOLTS

In order to become a National Board Certified Teacher (NBCT) practitioners must provide *clear, convincing, and consistent* evidence they have met the NB standards at an accomplished level. You show accomplishment by completing four portfolio entries and taking six 30-minute grade- and content-specific examinations. The four portfolio entries, worth 60 percent of the final score, and the six exams, worth 40 percent of the final score, together comprise the requirements. The portfolio instructions and assessment center topics are available on the NBPTS website: *www.nbpts.org*. Download the standards and instructions for the certificate you are attempting.

Three portfolio entries are based on student work, classroom videos, and other instructional artifacts. The fourth entry is about the work you do and have done to advance your professional learning; what you do to engage parents and the community as learning partners; and your collegial collaborations. The six assessment center exams concentrate on your content and grade-level knowledge. With everything you do for this certificate, the focus is always on student learning. The questions guiding you as you complete the portfolio entries will in themselves enrich your teaching practice, beginning with the portfolio structure.

The National Board uses the best standards-based instructional strategies in outlining the portfolio requirements. At the onset teacher-candidates know the specific standards for each certificate, the scoring guides by which their entries will be assessed, and the complete instructions for each portfolio entry. How does this structure compare to your teaching practice? Do students know in advance the standards they are expected to meet? Do they have a scoring guide specifying the criteria by which their accomplishments will be measured? Are your instructions to them clearly communicated and easy to follow?

COMPUTER SKILLS

All the portfolio entries, as well as the assessment center exercises, must be typed. How fast and how accurate you need to be varies, but at the very least you should be comfortable negotiating a word-processing document. I estimate that accurately typing forty-five words or more a minute, at a minimum, allows you to focus on the entries themselves without worrying about the mechanics. In the future, portfolio entries will be electronically submitted. Already, with few exceptions, the assessment center option of handwriting has been eliminated. And this is how it should be. If we are to prepare our students for successful participation in the 21st century, technology should be part of our practice. A teacher's comfort with basic computer functions—word-processing documents, Excel spreadsheets, email and the Internet, at minimum—transfers to students. Although I do know a few candidates who attempted certification by hiring typists or relying on friends and family, none were successful in their first attempt. If you need this year to become more computer savvy, it will be a year well spent. Certification can wait until you're ready.

THE FIVE CORE PROPOSITIONS

All the certificate standards are based on the five core propositions:

1. Teachers are committed to students and their learning.
2. Teachers know the subjects they teach and how to teach those subjects to students.
3. Teachers are responsible for managing and monitoring student learning.
4. Teachers think systematically about their practice and learn from experience.
5. Teachers are members of learning communities.

The full text for each of the propositions is available on the NBPTS website. Read them, analyze them, think about them, visualize how they appear in the most accomplished practice, and then rate your teaching against them. An in-depth analysis of each proposition is the heart of *The Teacher's Guide to National Board Certification: Unpacking the Standards*, the companion volume.

INSTRUCTIONS

☐ Use the personal inventory sheets appearing on the following pages as you examine your practice against the NB core propositions. Duplicate pages as needed.

☐ For each core proposition, note the key ideas as you understand them.

☐ Provide one or more specific examples of how this key idea looks in your practice.

☐ Note your areas of strength; the areas where you're weak.

☐ Determine what resources you might need to augment your current practice.

☐ Write down the steps you will take to become an accomplished teacher.

PERSONAL INVENTORY SHEET—EXAMPLE

CORE PROPOSITION 1: TEACHERS ARE COMMITTED TO STUDENTS AND THEIR LEARNING

KEY POINTS	CLEAR, CONSISTENT, AND CONVINCING EVIDENCE	POSSIBLE IMPROVEMENTS	NEXT STEPS
1. All students can learn.	I assess each child's current skill level to determine how best to help the child to continue learning.	I could learn more about how the brain learns.	Study *How People Learn*, from the National Research Council. Encourage a colleague to study how the brain learns with me.
2. Knowledge is made accessible.	I build on what students already know and add increments to their existing knowledge. I use strategies like KWL and reciprocal teaching to enhance learning.	Examine how I give instructions to make certain they are clear and accessible to all students.	Write out the instructions and ask a group of students to read them and provide feedback to me so I can improve my practice.
3. Students' lives have dignity.	I value students' home cultures and believe they each bring something of value to the classroom. Our classroom has a bulletin board with photos the students take of their neighborhood.	Project: Get disposable cameras so all students can take out-of-school pictures of their lives beyond the playground. Use these for talking points about cultural differences and similarities.	Investigate small grant to cover the cost of cameras for students. Contact PTA.
4. Student uniqueness is recognized.	Students are unique. Each is valued. When we write poetry, students select their own topics to write about.	Include more ways students can demonstrate accomplishment instead of the one or two options I usually provide. Include more differentiated instruction.	Check with other teachers how they provide differentiated instruction and multiple assessments.
5.			

Personal Inventory Worksheets

Core Proposition 1: Teachers are committed to students and their learning

Key Points	Clear, Consistent, and Convincing Evidence	Possible Improvements	Next Steps
1.			
2.			
3.			
4.			
5.			

Core Proposition 2: Teachers know the subjects they teach and how to teach those subjects to students

Key Points	Clear, Consistent, and Convincing Evidence	Possible Improvements	Next Steps
1.			
2.			
3.			
4.			
5.			

Core Proposition 3: Teachers are responsible for managing and monitoring student learning

Key Points	Clear, Consistent, and Convincing Evidence	Possible Improvements	Next Steps
1.			
2.			
3.			
4.			
5.			

8

Core Proposition 4: Teachers think systematically about their practice and learn from experience

Key Points	Clear, Consistent, and Convincing Evidence	Possible Improvements	Next Steps
1.			
2.			
3.			
4.			
5.			

Core Proposition 5: Teachers are members of learning communities

Key Points	Clear, Consistent, and Convincing Evidence	Possible Improvements	Next Steps
1.			
2.			
3.			
4.			
5.			

REFLECTION—BELIEFS ABOUT STUDENTS

REFLECTION

Because we teach based upon what we believe, it's important that we identify our core beliefs.

INSTRUCTIONS

I. Quickly list ten adjectives, words, or phrases you would use to describe your students. Don't do any editing yet, just list the ideas as they come to you.

☐
☐
☐
☐
☐
☐
☐
☐
☐
☐

II. Read your list. Based on how you've described your students, what do you believe about them? About their learning? About your role as their teacher? How do your beliefs impact your teaching? Your students' learning?

III. How do your current beliefs about your students match the National Board's core propositions? How do they vary? Why is this important?

IV. What evidence in your current practice demonstrates what you believe about your students and their learning?

V. What would your practice look like if you were completely committed to students and their learning as defined in the core propositions?

VI. Select two or more current or past students. How do they match with, or vary from, your beliefs as stated above? Why does this evaluation matter?

THE GLOSSARY AND
OTHER DEFINITIONS

Each set of portfolio instructions contains a glossary. Read through the glossary for definitions of education-related terms as they are used by the assessors. Many candidates forget that this is a national process. Bilingual education, for example, may be practiced and defined differently in North Carolina or Louisiana than it is in California. Because your entries and assessment exams are scored at various sites throughout the country, and by assessors who live and work in different parts of the country, it is critically important that we share common definitions. Use the definitions the National Board has provided in the glossary, even if you disagree with them!

Acronyms tend to be applied locally, not nationally. The first time you are explaining an organization or idea that has an acronym, write it out in full, followed by the acronym in parentheses. For all subsequent references you can then use the acronym only.

Follow the same procedure if you are defining a system, a program, or something you are doing at your site or in your district that may not be universally applicable. For instance, I worked at Center X. The first time I mentioned this in my portfolio entry on documented accomplishments I wrote, "Center X (The university department in which teaching practice and research intersected.)." In subsequent references I used Center X only. *Note:* I didn't put the name of the university because the portfolio instructions ask that we avoid using the name of a university whenever possible. See the portfolio instructions for details in the section *Naming Persons, Institutions, and Places.*

EXAMINING THE NATIONAL BOARD CERTIFICATE STANDARDS

Determine which certificate you wish to complete. At the time of this writing, there were twenty-four certificates covering approximately 95 percent of all teaching positions. Your choice depends on your current teaching assignment, not on your credential or major field of past college study. For example, you may have a math degree, but if you teach a self-contained first-grade class, your certificate is most likely the Early Childhood Generalist. However, you may have some additional choices. Do you teach English Language Learners? Students with Exceptional Needs? Are you an itinerant teacher? Do you specialize in art or music?

If you're unsure which certificate is best for you, go to the NB web page on standards at: *www.nbpts.org/standards/index.cfm.*

Read through the overviews and select the standards that most closely match your current teaching assignment. Still not certain? If you have more than one choice, i.e., you're teaching first grade but most of your students are English Language Learners, you may be eligible to apply for the Early Childhood Generalist or English as a New Language certificate. In which area do you feel most accomplished?

Still not sure? Open the PDF version of the portfolio instructions in the certificates you are considering. For each certificate, read the overview found around page 27. (The page number may vary slightly for each certificate.) Given your current assignment, could you complete each entry for this certificate?

Once you have determined which certificate you will be working with, download the complete standards document, or, if you prefer, you can order the standards booklet at 1-800-22TEACH for $15 each. Delivery takes approximately two weeks.

Now it's time for a very personal inventory against the NB certificate standards. We'll use the same technique we used for examining the core propositions, only these standards represent accomplished teaching in your grade level or field. Do a complete inventory for each standard in your certificate area. Just as in the core propositions, the standards overlap. You'll find key points in one that are similar to key points in another. You be the judge of how detailed you want this inventory to be. The more preparation and self-analysis you do now, the easier it will be to analyze your teaching later on. Remember that to achieve National Board Certification you must provide clear, convincing, and consistent evidence that you have met the standards at an accomplished level. The better you know the standards, the more you have absorbed what they say, what they mean, and why they matter, the better will be your choices as you complete the portfolio entries.

Preparation time is time well spent. As you're making note of the key points, closely examine the language of the standards. Pay attention to the active verbs. Highlight them. Weave the language of the standards into your entry. Complete an individual inventory for each standard in your certificate. Duplicate the inventory forms as needed.

Some teachers become very defensive while completing these personal inventories. They have a way of teaching they're comfortable with and resent when someone or something suggests there is another way. I am convinced, as are many other educators, that because the National Board has carefully developed the standards for each certificate with primary input from classroom teachers, that these standards do represent best teaching practices. If, as you examine these standards and measure your practice against them, you find particular areas that cause you discomfort, or with which you absolutely disagree, that's a great place to stop for reflection or to join with colleagues in discussion.

Keep in mind that the National Board Standards are for accomplished teachers and will differ significantly, in their depth and breadth, from the standards for new teachers many of us are familiar with in our work as mentors. The National Board has raised the standards for the profession. Where do you measure up? Where do you need to stretch and grow?

STANDARDS PERSONAL INVENTORY SHEET—EXAMPLE

CERTIFICATE: __MC GENERALIST__ STANDARD: __III. LEARNING ENVIRONMENT__

KEY POINTS	*CLEAR, CONSISTENT, AND CONVINCING EVIDENCE*	POSSIBLE IMPROVEMENTS	NEXT STEPS
1. Physical safety of students	Scissors and supplies are stored safely in a closet. Children don't run when they have scissors.		
2. Emotional safety of students	No one is allowed to put down, or make any insulting remarks to, another student or to the teacher. The teacher treats students respectfully.		
3. Teacher demonstrates interest in students' lives	There is a hobby board where students post notes and pictures of themselves in their out-of-school play.	Project: Get disposable cameras so all students can take out-of-school pictures of their lives beyond the playground. Use these for talking points.	Investigate small grant to cover the cost of cameras for students. Contact PTA.
4. Fairness in grouping practices	Students are grouped for a variety of activities. Some groups are done randomly so no child is left out.	Read about grouping practices and their impact on student learning.	Check the Google website for grouping practices. Check with other teachers.
5.			

STANDARDS PERSONAL INVENTORY WORKSHEETS

CERTIFICATE: _____

STANDARD: _____

KEY POINTS	CLEAR, CONSISTENT, AND CONVINCING EVIDENCE	POSSIBLE IMPROVEMENTS	NEXT STEPS
1.			
2.			
3.			
4.			
5.			

CERTIFICATE: _____ STANDARD: _____

KEY POINTS	CLEAR, CONSISTENT, AND CONVINCING EVIDENCE	POSSIBLE IMPROVEMENTS	NEXT STEPS
1.			
2.			
3.			
4.			
5.			

CERTIFICATE: _____   STANDARD: _____

KEY POINTS	CLEAR, CONSISTENT, AND CONVINCING EVIDENCE	POSSIBLE IMPROVEMENTS	NEXT STEPS
1.			
2.			
3.			
4.			
5.			

22

CERTIFICATE: _____ STANDARD: _____

KEY POINTS	CLEAR, CONSISTENT, AND CONVINCING EVIDENCE	POSSIBLE IMPROVEMENTS	NEXT STEPS
1.			
2.			
3.			
4.			
5.			

CLASSROOM LAYOUT AND LEARNING ENVIRONMENT REFLECTIONS

For each of the videotaped entries you will be asked to provide a sketch of your classroom layout to give the assessors a sense of the physical layout of your room. Your classroom layout is also an excellent way to reflect on your teaching practice. Each certificate has standards related to the learning environment. Now that you have read the standards and completed your personal inventories, let's combine the classroom layout and the standards.

Given the physical constraints of your classroom, why have you chosen to arrange the room the way you have? How does this room arrangement contribute to student learning? How well does this arrangement allow for student access to materials and books? Does the room arrangement accommodate students with special needs? Does the room arrangement allow for interaction between you and each student? Between students? What changes, if any, would best promote student and teacher learning?

EXAMINING THE PORTFOLIO ENTRIES 1–4*

INSTRUCTIONS

☐ Download the portfolio instructions, if you haven't already done so. The instructions can be found on the NB website: *www.nbpts.org/candidates/portfolios.cfm*

☐ Put the instructions into a binder. Use dividers to separate each section; this will save you lots of time later when you're navigating through the instructions.

☐ Go to the section with the portfolio entry requirements.

☐ For each entry, read the instructions carefully. If you're working with one or more colleagues, you may each want to read the instructions independently and then compare your notes. Enter the entry requirements on the following page: The Portfolio Overview. This will enable you to see at a glance the complete portfolio requirements. Condensing the instructions from the 200-plus-page document to one graphic organizer makes the whole process seem more doable—and it is.

*Entry 4 will be examined in depth as it is basically the same for all certificates and a great place to get started.

THE PORTFOLIO OVERVIEW

CERTIFICATE _____

	ENTRY NAME	THE STANDARDS ADDRESSED	TYPE OF EVIDENCE REQUIRED	NUMBER OF STUDENTS	TIME PERIOD COVERED IN THIS ENTRY	HOW DOES THIS ENTRY CHALLENGE ME?
Portfolio Entry 1						
Portfolio Entry 2						
Portfolio Entry 3						
Portfolio Entry 4						

REFLECTION—CHALLENGES AND SUPPORTS

REFLECTION
What are the challenges you anticipate as you work toward achieving National Board Certification? What fears, if any, do you have? What are the supports you have or can put in place?

Remember: **FEAR** is nothing more than: **False Expectations that Appear Real.**

TIME MANAGEMENT

Beginning with the 2002–2003 candidate-year the National Board has opened the time period during which candidates may apply for certification. All candidates have a twelve-month cycle in which to complete the initial portfolio entries and assessment center exercises. An additional twenty-four months is allowed for retake entries, if needed. Candidates are advised to select the cycle that best fits their teaching calendar and personal time commitments. Depending on which cycle you as the candidate select, you may submit lessons and student work from one school year or you may elect to use lessons and student work from two consecutive school years.

The cycle is determined by your initial payment of $300 to the National Board. However, you no longer have to apply to the National Board to begin working on the portfolio entries. I recommend that you download the standards and portfolio instructions and begin your analysis prior to applying to the National Board. Once you've begun analyzing your practice and determining how much time you'll need to successfully complete the Board requirements, you can then determine the best time to begin the cycle. You may find, as do some of the teachers who work with me, that an additional six months or year of groundwork, prior to submitting your official application, will better prepare you for this rigorous, high-stakes, assessment process.

The following monthly timeline is intended as a guide only. You will note that there are several references to working with a cohort group, colleagues who are working toward Board certification along with you. Candidates benefit by working with others. Committed colleagues read the drafts of your entries, offer suggestions when you get stuck, and encourage you when you are thinking of quitting. The portfolio entries and standards are excellent texts around which to have meaningful and productive professional discussions. Take advantage of this process to continue your learning. A discussion about cohort groups appears elsewhere in this workbook.

Teachers often think they have to reinvent teaching. The National Board encourages you to collaborate, to share ideas and lessons. You don't have to submit original lessons or activities, just effective ones. If you work with a colleague, team-teach, share students and/or lessons, say so in your entry. You will not lose points for collaboration. The National Board promotes teacher collaboration. However, the student work you submit must be a result of your teaching.

Perhaps the greatest challenge my candidates face is one of time management. To get the most benefit from this professional development process it is important to allow sufficient time for analysis, writing, reflection, revision, more analysis, and more reflection. Rushing through the portfolio entries or arriving ill prepared to the assessment center not only increases the stress level, but also reduces your chances to achieve certification. Plan your time well. Eliminate activities that are not productive, that take a disproportionate amount of energy from you. Disassociate from those people who drain your energy, and increase your time with others who give you energy. Optimistic, "I can do it" colleagues are a joy; whiners are just that, whiners. While it's true that at schools, as in other organizations, 20 percent of the people do 80 percent of the work, and you're probably in the 20 percent, your candidacy year is a time for you to be a little selfish. Choose carefully how and where you'll spend your time. The suggested timeline included in this workbook is based on six years of experience as a candidate and support provider for more than 700 candidates.

Twenty-three hundred dollars in National Board fees is a considerable investment. The fees are used to offset the cost of reading, viewing, and scoring candidate entries. If even the day before you are scheduled to submit your portfolio entries or to take the assessment center tests, you decide that you are not ready, that your portfolio does not demonstrate accomplishment, you can withdraw and get a $2,000 refund. Once you either submit the portfolio or take the assessment center tests, you are an official candidate and your fees are forfeited. The withdrawal form is available at the NB website.

Ask yourself: Can you find time for the National Board process and still do the things you need to do? What can you reduce or eliminate? Don't forget to keep some time for personal renewal and rejuvenation. You know the old adage about all work and no play; it applies here as well.

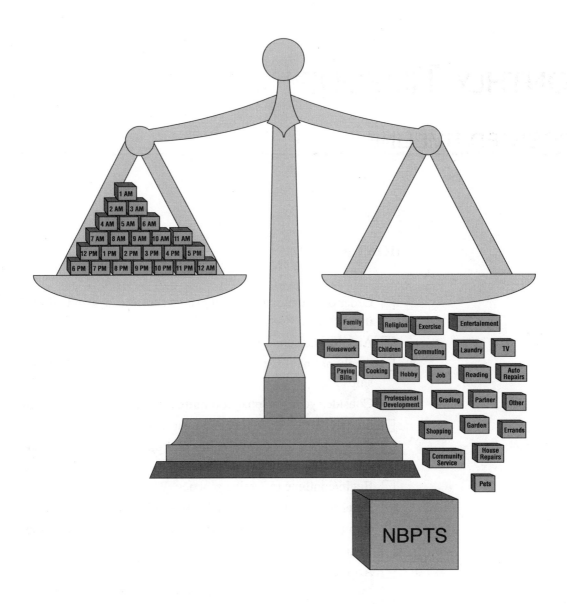

**Can you balance your available time and
all you want to accomplish?**

MONTHLY TIMELINE

SUGGESTED TIMELINE

MONTH 1

- ☑ Order or download [*www.nbpts.org*] certificate standards and portfolio instructions.
- ☑ Arrange fee support.
- ☐ Apply online for state subsidy, if available, and other possible scholarships.
- ☐ Consider your personal commitments and adjust accordingly.
- ☐ Study NBPTS Standards and Instructions.
- ☐ Complete personal inventories and plan to strengthen areas of weakness or challenge.
- ☑ Begin/continue reflective practice. Write in a journal.
- ☐ Determine cycle for NBPTS certification process.
- ☐ Complete the Portfolio Entries–Overview for all four entries.
- ☐ Begin Entry 4.
- ☐ Arrange for videotaping equipment.
- ☐ Meet with your professional learning cohort.
- ☐ Establish student portfolios (one method for collecting student work).

MONTH 2

- ☐ Apply online for National Board Certification.
- ☐ Select or continue with your cohort group meetings.
- ☐ Establish group norms; calendar meeting times and places.
- ☐ Examine student work to improve teaching and learning.
  - ○ Go to: *www.google.com*, then to *LASW* for protocols for examining student work.
  - ○ Practice discussing student work using the Reflective Conversation Questions included later in this workbook.

The National Board Certification Workbook

- [x] Select students (more than required) and possible lessons for entries.
- [ ] Check your entries' overview to establish/review your time schedule for entries.
- [ ] Establish/maintain student portfolios.
- [ ] Plan/implement family and community outreach activities.
- [ ] Continue journaling as reflective practice.
- [x] Videotape one or two classes. Watch with your students. Transcribe.
- [ ] Notify your students/families about what you are doing this year. Ask for their support.
- [x] Get signed student/adult release forms. Release forms in fourteen languages are available without charge from the National Board: 1-800-22TEACH.
- [ ] Share/exchange/write cover letters to go with release forms.
- [x] Describe the context of your teaching environment. Get data from Dataquest, if available in your state, and from school site. See *http://data1.cde.ca.gov/dataquest/,* for example.
- [ ] Bring student work to your group for examination and analysis.

MONTH 3

NOV
DEC

- [ ] Study the Glossary of Terms included with the portfolio instructions.
- [ ] Practice videotaping.
- [ ] Transcribe video paying careful attention to questioning techniques.
- [ ] Overcome technical difficulties.
- [ ] Analyze what you see in the video.
- [ ] Share with your group.
- [ ] Write draft of video entry
- [ ] Continue journaling as reflective practice.
- [ ] Draft Entry 4. Check for gaps. Plan to fill in gaps.
- [ ] Continue to examine student work to inform instruction.
- [ ] Consider/develop/use rubrics/scoring guides.

MONTH 4

DEC

- [ ] Complete penultimate draft of Entry 4.
- [ ] Select/confirm/teach lessons for portfolio entries.
- [ ] Draft second entry.
- [ ] Continue reflective practice.

MONTH 5

JAN

- ☐ Complete Entry 4.
- ☐ Complete second entry.
- ☐ Draft last two entries.
- ☐ Share with colleagues.

MONTH 6

Feb

- ☐ Complete draft of all entries.
- ☐ Share with colleagues.
- ☐ Score entries against the standards.
- ☐ Revise entries.

MONTH 7

March

- ☐ Revise/complete entries and compile all documentation.
- ☐ Edit and proofread.
- ☐ Fill gaps, if any.
- ☐ Mail portfolio entries.
- ☐ Make appointment for assessment center.

MONTH 8

- ☐ Prepare for assessment center.
- ☐ Take practice timed tests.
- ☐ Complete Assessment Center exercises.
- ☐ Relax/celebrate/begin waiting.

WAITING FOR SCORES

- ☐ Celebrate yourself.
- ☐ Refresh and renew.
- ☐ Wait.
- ☐ Celebrate your accomplishment.

COLLABORATION AND COHORT GROUPS

Many NB candidates go it alone, but we don't have any official statistics on how many or on how successful they are. I do know, from my extensive experience, that candidates who work in dedicated cohort groups have a significantly higher chance of achieving certification. I waited nearly two years from the time I first became interested in certification until I was able to entice some colleagues to join me in this professional endeavor. I knew that the experience would be richer for me if I shared it with others. Of our original group of eighteen, 50 percent certified the first year at a time when the certification rate nationally was hovering under 35 percent, and all but one certified on the second attempt. More importantly, we learned so much from one another during the months we worked together. There is an excitement and energy that develops among dedicated teachers working on a common goal that is rarely matched in the faculty lounge or any other professional setting.

The candidate support program I direct meets for four days to begin the NB process, and then monthly as a K–12 facilitated group. Candidates are strongly encouraged to meet with small (four- to six-member) cohort groups in between the monthly meetings. These are the colleagues who will read each of your entries, nurture you as you probe your practice, encourage you when you feel overwhelmed, and help you to stick to the timeline. By the end of the NB process you will have bonded. (The children of two of my candidates who participated in the same cohort group met and married!) Teachers who work collaboratively vow they will never work in isolation again.

Six years ago, when I began this work, I thought all I needed to do was put four teachers around a table and they would immediately be collaborative. (Isn't that what we often do in our classrooms?) Some groups did work well from the outset, but most didn't. Since then I always take time to teach collaborative practices. Although I'm working with teachers, all these practices can move into the classroom. Here's a step-by-step method that works well when forming working groups.

First, begin with a personal learning reflection:

WRITE FIVE ENDINGS FOR THIS SENTENCE:

I LEARN BEST WHEN . . .

- ☐
- ☐
- ☐
- ☐
- ☐

NOW WRITE FIVE ENDINGS FOR THIS SENTENCE:

I DON'T LEARN WELL WHEN . . .

- ☐
- ☐
- ☐
- ☐
- ☐

You'll want to form a cohort group with others who share similar learning styles, or who are flexible enough to adapt to one another. If one learns best with loud music blasting and you demand absolute quiet, you're probably not a good match. In addition to learning style you may want to consider colleagues who are working on the same certificate, who teach at the same school or one nearby, who live near you, or who like to meet on Saturday mornings, or who will never meet on Saturday mornings. Once you've gathered agreeable colleagues, take the time to establish some group norms.

Determine the five norms your group believes are essential for a strong professional learning community. Engage in a discussion around each member's beliefs, then write down what you agree to. (For the classroom, what would happen if instead of class rules you and your students established classroom norms essential for promoting academic success?)

SUGGESTED SIMPLE RULES FOR EFFECTIVE COHORT GROUPS

1. Agree to a regularly scheduled meeting place and time.
2. Be prompt—arrive on time.
3. Be prepared with the assignment the group agreed upon at the previous session. Use the timeline as a guide.
4. Be productive—stay focused on the issue(s) addressed during each cohort meeting. Don't waste time whining about things you can't control. Focus on your teaching and student learning.
5. Be polite—respectful of one another's feelings, teaching context, and challenges.
6. Stay committed to one another. You're in this for the long haul.

During your period of candidacy, especially working in small cohort groups, you'll be sharing your writing, your students' work, your strengths and your weaknesses. For many candidates, this is the first time they will be working so intimately with colleagues. Sharing involves risk-taking. This is not about a teacher saying I do this or I do that in my classroom, but about examining what the students do as a result of what the teacher does. We share best in a physically and emotionally safe atmosphere. Teachers, and students, are more willing to take intellectual risks when they know their audience is committed to listening in an active and respectful manner. What follows is a guide for promoting thoughtful, safe questioning of one another's practice, while helping to uncover, and recover, what is happening in our classrooms and with our students. *Remember:* the techniques that work well with teachers, work equally well with students.

First, the basics:

BEGIN WITH *POSITIVE PRESUPPOSITIONS:*

☐ Assume the speaker has good intentions in the work he or she does with students/others.
☐ Carefully pose the questions you ask to assure there are no hidden negatives.
   ○ Example: There's a difference between asking: *What were you thinking when you did that?* and *What was your rationale/reason for choosing that strategy with this lesson?*
☐ Avoid causing your colleagues to shut down.

WE POSE QUESTIONS IN ORDER TO

☐ Promote analytical and reflective thinking
☐ Encourage articulation of thoughts
☐ Uncover things we know, and things we don't know
☐ Push ourselves to explore our learning more deeply

PARAPHRASING IS

☐ A restatement by the listener of what he or she understood
☐ Not an alteration of the speaker's intent
☐ A summary of what the listener heard
☐ A prompt for the speaker to restate, or explain, if the listener needs more clarification

PROBING AND CLARIFYING QUESTIONS

☐ Are posed when the audience doesn't understand
☐ Are used when the audience needs more information
☐ Help speakers to extend the information
☐ Help us to interpret our practice more deeply

REFLECTIVE CONVERSATION QUESTIONS

☐ Serve as effective sentence starters

☐ Focus us on the work before us, not the personality of the presenter

☐ Are sensitive to others' vulnerability

☐ Are not magic, but are helpful in promoting safe learning environments

☐ Can be altered or abandoned as the group becomes more comfortable with one another

I've learned all the above techniques from a variety of sources, some from the National Board training itself. While I would like to give credit where it is due, I'm not sure I could assign any one idea to any one original source. Therefore, I wish to publicly acknowledge the many colleagues who have contributed to my own learning, to the National Board, to WestEd and other education groups, formal and informal.

The reflective conversation questions that follow work especially well for any group, teachers or students, examining one another's writing. I suggest that members of the group read the sentence starters aloud before they begin using them. It may seem a little artificial, but it is a way to exercise the tongue, to get it used to using the sentence starters. These sentence starters will actually help you stay away from some of the pitfalls I'll describe later.

REFLECTIVE CONVERSATION QUESTIONS

Use as sentence starters.

PARAPHRASING

So . . .
In other words . . .
What I'm hearing then . . .
What I hear you saying . . .
From what I hear you say . . .
I'm hearing many things . . .
As I listen to you I'm hearing . . .

CLARIFYING

Would you tell me a little more about . . .
Let me see if I understand . . .
I'd be interested in hearing more about . . .
It'd help me understand if you'd give me an example of . . .
So, are you saying/suggesting . . .?
Tell me what you mean when you . . .
Tell me how that idea is like (different from) . . .
To what extent . . .?
I'm curious to know more about . . .
I'm intrigued by . . .
I'm interested in . . .
I wonder . . .

MEDIATIONAL

What's another way you might . . .?

What would it look like if . . .?

What do you think would happen if . . .?

How was . . . different from (like) . . .?

What sort of an impact do you think . . .?

What criteria do you use to . . .?

When have you done something like . . . before?

What do you think . . . ?

How did you decide . . . (come to that conclusion)?

What might you see happening in your classroom if . . .?

WORKING WITH THE COHORT GROUP

Okay, you've formed your cohort, you've established your group norms, and now you're ready to work. Much of the work you do together this year will be examining your written portfolio entries and viewing and analyzing one another's videotapes.

There are many protocols you can use to examine one another's entries and tapes. Most groups benefit from beginning with a structured protocol while they are getting used to working with one another, and then abandon it once trust is established. Check out the Internet for other examples, or use the one included in this workbook—it works.

LOOKING AT TEACHERS' WORK—A PROTOCOL

INSTRUCTIONS

For this protocol we'll use the reflective conversation questions. Take a few minutes with your cohort group to read aloud the reflective conversation questions so they are fresh in your mind. Remember as you examine one another's work to *presume good intentions*. The purpose is to provide constructive feedback without causing others to shut down or become defensive. For ease of explanation I've used entries as the focus of the task. You can easily substitute a video or student work for the portfolio entry.

1. Select a facilitator whose job it is to make sure the group stays focused on the entry/video/student work.

2. Select a timekeeper. The timekeeper divides the allotted time by the number of candidates whose entry will be reviewed so everyone has an equal amount of time.

3. Each group member has a hard copy of the candidate's entry, or part of the entry, whatever the group has decided.

4. The presenting candidate reads the entry draft. Everyone listens. The presenting candidate reads the entry a second time; this time group members note the key ideas the entry addresses. Members should also note areas for clarification, where they want additional information, etc. These notes become the talking points.

5. After reading the draft twice, the presenting candidate remains silent. *Listen, don't be defensive.* The group members discuss the entry—always keeping in mind this is a draft. The facilitator can direct the questioning or allow it to flow naturally. This is the time to ask for clarification, to state which standards were addressed and which were not.

6. Following the facilitated discussion, each group member makes a final comment. Group members may ask for clarification, and additions, make recommendations, and give commendations. Comments like "That's great" or "What a terrific activity" don't help the candidate. However, "That's great" followed by a specific reference to the entry and its connection to the key points you've identified when you did your standards inventory can be valuable. Other helpful comments include: "I didn't know what you meant by _____; could you explain more fully?"

7. Repeat Steps 3–6 for each candidate.

Avoid the pitfalls of trying to solve teaching problems, or change the teaching, or suggesting other strategies to use for the lesson. Those are great items to discuss, at another time, or later during the meeting. For this part of the group session, it's important to focus on what the candidate wrote—the content of the draft. Did the entry address the standards? Did the candidate follow the instructions? Does this work represent accomplished teaching? Although the candidate always makes the final decision about what should or should not be included, feedback from the group is invaluable. If all are saying the same thing about clarity, choice, or anything else, it's worth listening. I've never had candidates tell me that they didn't benefit from working with their group.

Note: This protocol is like a script. Use it if it assists you in accomplishing the goal. The goal is to document clearly your teaching practice in response to the guiding questions included in the portfolio instructions for each entry. Discard the protocol in part or in whole if you find that it hampers the process rather than aids it.

It is really important to remember that when you send your portfolio to the Board, you won't have the luxury of sitting on the assessor's shoulder and clarifying or adding to anything you've written. The portfolio entry stands alone. Here's why having an audience beyond yourself, an audience of candidates who have a personal investment in your success, as you have in theirs, is so valuable. Pretend that each member of your cohort group represents an assessor. What they understand, the assessor will most likely understand. What you write, how clearly and fully you analyze your teaching practices, will help the assessor to score your entry accurately. Make it easy. Write clearly and concisely, follow the instructions, respond to the guiding questions, address the standards, and include all the required attachments.

AM I READY FOR NATIONAL BOARD CERTIFICATION?

Before making any further commitments, like applying to the National Board and sending your application fee, telling your family you are not going to cook or take out the trash for the next year while you're completing your portfolio, take the time for this reflective quiz. Be flexible as the answers may not quite line up with the Leikert scale, but since this is between you and you, and not for research analysis, precision won't matter.

1	Absolutely Not
2	Not Likely
3	Maybe
4	Probably
5	Absolutely Can Do

CONSIDERATION	SCALE
1. I have 200–400 hours of professional time during this year to devote to this process.	1 2 3 4 5
2. I am a self-starter and self-motivated.	1 2 3 4 5
3. I view myself as a teacher who maintains high standards for myself and sets high expectations for my students.	1 2 3 4 5

CONSIDERATION	SCALE				
	1	2	3	4	5
4. I have examined the five core propositions and completed my personal inventory.					
5. I have examined the standards for my certificate and completed my personal inventory.					
6. I have examined Entries 1, 2, 3 and 4 and can successfully complete each of them.					
7. I can provide evidence (according to the NB definition) of accomplished teaching.					
8. I have significant evidence of my Documented Accomplishments available in accordance with Entry 4.					
9. I regularly reflect upon and modify my teaching practices.					
10. I work well with colleagues.					
11. I look forward to sharing and discussing my students' work.					

CONSIDERATION	SCALE				
12. I welcome the comments of other teachers about my written work.	1	2	3	4	5
13. I welcome the comments of other teachers about my practice.	1	2	3	4	5
14. I look forward to sharing my classroom videos with my cohort group.	1	2	3	4	5
15. I can attend scheduled after-school monthly meetings (if or when they are scheduled).	1	2	3	4	5
16. I can meet on a regular basis with my cohort group.	1	2	3	4	5
17. I can travel, if necessary, to meetings in various parts of the city.	1	2	3	4	5
18. I can attend workshops, if necessary, to deepen my knowledge base.	1	2	3	4	5
19. My family/friends will act as a support system for me.	1	2	3	4	5
20. I can limit my personal activities to provide the time I will need.	1	2	3	4	5

CONSIDERATION	SCALE				
21. My current school administration will support my candidacy (emotional support, video equipment, release time, etc.)	1	2	3	4	5
22. I can say no when asked to join still another school committee, or chair another school function.	1	2	3	4	5
23. I am computer literate and have email and Internet access.	1	2	3	4	5
24. I can arrange to pay the $2,300 NB fees, if necessary.	1	2	3	4	5
25. I am not a procrastinator. I can follow the suggested timeline or create one I will follow.	1	2	3	4	5
26. I am already an accomplished teacher.	1	2	3	4	5

Now add up your scores. If you're at 65 or below, you should most likely wait a while. In the 65–80 range, it doesn't sound like you have a strong commitment, yet. A score of 80–100 is looking good. More than 100, what are you waiting for?

Of course, this is not a scientific survey, just a useful tool some friends and I came up with. I thank Diana Cotter of Los Angeles Unified and the hundreds of teachers who have shared these questions with me.

REFLECTION—AM I READY

This is it. You are beginning the National Board process, approximately ten months of describing, analyzing, and reflecting on your teaching practice. Where are you going to find the time? How are you going to do it all? What activities are you planning to reduce or cut out? How will you organize your time? Your space for working? What scares you? Excites you? What are your burning concerns, if any?

CONTEXTUAL INFORMATION AND THE INSTRUCTIONAL CONTEXT

National Board certification is not a competitive enterprise. There are no quotas limiting the number of teachers who can become certified. Teachers are not matched one against another with the *best* achieving certification and the *rest* left behind. All teacher candidates who provide clear, convincing, and consistent evidence of achieving the applicable standards achieve certification. Even though the standards are applicable for all candidates, there remain wide variations between teaching environments. The assessors are thoroughly familiar with the standards for the certificate they are scoring, but it is up to the individual candidates to provide an accurate picture of their professional environment in order for assessors to score candidates' entries accurately. The Board seeks this information in two ways.

First, candidates are asked to describe the broader context in which they teach. Contextual Information may include the school district size and setting (rural, suburban, or urban), student ethnographic information, socioeconomic factors, district and/or schoolwide language diversity and competence, transient and dropout rates, and state and district mandates that impact teaching choices. Candidates are encouraged to provide sufficient *relevant* information to provide the assessors with a clear picture of their teaching context. For candidates teaching in only one school, they complete this information once and include the same information with each entry. For the few candidates who may teach in more than one school, they complete the contextual information for each different school setting.

The Contextual Information is about the big picture of your teaching environment, whereas the Instructional Context focuses on the classroom you are featuring in a particular entry. If you teach an all-day self-contained class, you may write this description one time and duplicate it for each entry. If the class you highlight differs from one entry to the next, as is frequently the case for secondary teachers, you write a separate description of the Contextual Information for each featured class. The Instructional Context description should include all the features *relevant* to your instructional choices. This information might include the number and ages of students, their ethnic, linguistic, and cultural diversity, their ability range, social and behavioral considerations, special needs of designated students, and anything else that would define the personality of the featured class. Include the particular challenges this class presents.

State and district mandates are increasing. If you are required to prepare students for standardized testing in a prescribed manner, mention it here. If you must use a language arts, math, or other program that is scripted or highly structured, mention it here. Try to be as objective as possible in your comments. It is not to your advantage to complain about the mandates, or to launch into a diatribe berating the policy makers, or even to voice strong support in favor of the mandates. State them in as objective a manner as possible. Avoid whining about all the things outsiders impose on teachers. The assessors are educators also and will understand the context if you state it clearly for them.

As with the rest of the NB process, gathering and analyzing this information may be important for the assessors, but it is even more important that teachers know and understand their teaching environments. We should make instructional choices based on an analysis of the available information and an understanding of our entire teaching context. Each class in each year of my twelve years in the classroom presented different challenges; students' needs changed, their ability levels fluctuated, the community's expectations increased. And each year my own knowledge level and range of available strategies grew. All this impacted my instructional choices. Accomplished teachers don't deliver *canned* lessons devoid of consideration of students' needs and abilities or free from consideration of the teaching context.

The Contextual Information sheet is included in the portfolio instructions. Your response must fit in the small spaces provided. Be sure to address the prompts. You may single-space on this sheet only.

> **Example** *I teach in a year-round, multitrack urban high school located on the fringe of a large city. The enrollment is 5,200 students in grades 9 through 12. The ethnic breakdown is as follows: 70% Hispanic, 12% African American, 9% Caucasian, 2% Native American Indian, 3% Asian, and 4% other. 80% of our students receive free or reduced lunch. 74% of the students are English Language Learners. The school is departmentalized by subject with no official interdisciplinary teams. The average class size is 30 but my 9th-grade classes are limited to 20 students each.*

The Instructional Context differs from the Contextual Information in that it focuses on the class featured in the entry. You may feature a different class for each of the three entries, or use the same one. You may also choose to use the same class, but highlight different *relevant* characteristics of the class for each entry.

> **Example** *I teach 5 periods of 9th-grade English Language Arts, 3 classes designated regular and 2 classes designated honors. I don't differentiate, but hold all students to high standards. This is a community that values math and science more*

*than Language Arts. The state mandate supports small class
sizes for 9th-grade English so I have only 100 students daily.
We have mandated standards that I must address; however,
these are general statements of what students know and are
able to do, so my curricula choices are mostly up to me. A
particular challenge is the range of cultural backgrounds, the
language development levels, and the different literacy abilities and skill levels students have upon entering my classes.
The school administration values quiet, orderly classrooms,
while I value discussion and interaction. In addition to the
curricula to address the standards, I prepare my students for
the Spring standardized tests by devoting two weeks to test-
prep exercises as mandated by the district.*

I've intentionally highlighted the word *relevant* in the preceding para-
graphs about contextual information and instructional context. A feature is
relevant, and should be included in your descriptions, if it impacts your
teaching choices. For example, if students have different cultural backgrounds and you include multicultural materials in your instructional
choices, then you would include that feature in your description.

Caution: I have read entries wherein candidates displayed an accurate
and thorough knowledge of the district and school demographics and used
the students' accumulated education records to accurately compile a class
profile. These candidates do an excellent job of setting the stage for the
assessor to understand the candidate's teaching context. But it is insufficient
to know the characteristics of your teaching context if you don't put that
knowledge to good use. When the candidate connects the relevant characteristics of the teaching context to the instructional choices, evidence of student achievement usually follows. But if a candidate describes students'
needs and then ignores those needs when making instructional choices, the
assessors don't see evidence of accomplished teaching. In fact, if after writing a description of the contextual information and the instructional context,
you discover that you have not addressed some of the identified students'
needs in your analysis of the featured lesson and the student work, then you
might want to consider omitting some of the characteristics you mentioned.

Failure to use the information about your school setting and/or students
to impact instructional decisions is worse than not knowing about your students at all. An accomplished teacher does not intentionally ignore an identified student need or strength. What follows from increased knowledge is
increased differentiated instruction. If you are going to describe contextual
features and instructional context, it is important to specifically reference, in
the body of your entry, how your instruction or choice of strategies
addressed this characteristic.

Draft the Contextual Information and Instructional Context sheets and
ask other educators, preferably from outside of your school, to read and

comment. Reflective conversation questions, included elsewhere in this workbook, can be used as a protocol to guide the critique. Remember, the purpose of these two sections is to set the stage so the assessors examine your teaching practice as it relates to your teaching context, not to an idealized version of what school should look like (one we often see in the movies) but how it actually is where you teach.

EFFECTIVE PRACTICES

The National Board doesn't tell you what to do or what not to do in your classroom. It does, however, ask you to identify your instructional goals and the strategies you use to help your students meet those goals. Accomplished teachers command a wide range of teaching strategies and know how and when to use them. The following checklist has been included as a reference only. It is not an exhaustive list of teaching strategies. You may know many of these practices by other names. If you find that you don't have a wide range of strategies, you might want to search out information, workshops, colleagues who know and effectively use strategies you are not familiar with. Seek professional development opportunities that will enrich your practice. We know that there is no single set of strategies effective with all students. Therefore, it is critically important that we come to the classroom prepared with multiple strategies so we can address the needs of all our students in the most effective ways possible.

EFFECTIVE TEACHING: STRATEGIES IDENTIFIED WITH STUDENT GAINS*

Effective teachers regularly use a variety of strategies. Depending on the instructional goal, effective teachers select specific strategies to help students to achieve the goals. The list of strategies that follows is not meant to be exhaustive. It does, however, include those strategies shown to be most effective in aiding student learning. *The NB portfolio instructions ask you to identify your instructional goals and the strategies you use to assist students in achieving those goals.*

For each of the strategies listed below rate how often you use the strategy.

1	Never
2	Seldom
3	Sometimes
4	Frequently
5	Very Frequently

STRATEGY	SCALE
1. Begin a lesson with a short review of previous learning; connect to future lessons/units; make interdisciplinary connections.	1 2 3 4 5
2. Begin a lesson with a short statement of instructional goals.	1 2 3 4 5
3. Make connections to the standard(s).	1 2 3 4 5
4. Give clear and detailed instructions and explanations.	1 2 3 4 5

STRATEGY	SCALE				
5. Ask a large number of questions, check for student understanding, and obtain responses from all students.	1	2	3	4	5
6. Present new material in small steps, providing for student practice after each step.	1	2	3	4	5
7. Provide for high-level student practice.	1	2	3	4	5
8. Guide students during initial practice.	1	2	3	4	5
9. Monitor students during seatwork.	1	2	3	4	5
10. Check for and correct student misconceptions.	1	2	3	4	5
11. Provide feedback in a timely manner (48 hours or less for graded work) from teacher, other students, on computers.	1	2	3	4	5
12. Teach students to generate questions at all levels.	1	2	3	4	5
13. Employ think-aloud strategies as a model/scaffold for students.	1	2	3	4	5
14. Allow time for student thinking about their thinking and learning (metacognition).	1	2	3	4	5
15. Reflect on your teaching effectiveness.	1	2	3	4	5
16. Scaffold tasks through modeling and/or cue cards or checklists, until students achieve mastery.	1	2	3	4	5

STRATEGY	SCALE				
17. Provide procedural prompts, such as sentence starters. (How are _____ and _____ alike? What is the main idea of _____?)	1	2	3	4	5
18. Provide models of sample responses.	1	2	3	4	5
19. Anticipate and discuss potential difficulties.	1	2	3	4	5
20. Regulate the difficulty of the task.	1	2	3	4	5
21. Provide and teach a checklist or scoring guide (rubric).	1	2	3	4	5
22. Provide independent practice with new examples.	1	2	3	4	5
23. Increase student responsibilities (never do what a student can—and should—do).	1	2	3	4	5
24. Help students to organize new material (graphic organizers, mind-mapping).	1	2	3	4	5
25. Use standards-based student portfolios with time for student analysis, reflection, and self-assessment.	1	2	3	4	5
26. Examine student work to improve your teaching effectiveness.	1	2	3	4	5

*These strategies are loosely adapted from Rosenshine and Stevens. Additions are drawn from my teaching experiences.

epaa.asu.edu/barak/barak/html

Rosenshine, B., and Stevens, R. (1986). Teaching Functions. In M. C. Wittrock (Ed.). *Handbook of Research on Teaching* (376–391). New York: Macmillan.

EFFECTIVE TEACHING—
ANALYSIS AND REFLECTION

☐ Select one of the strategies from the preceding checklist on Effective Teaching on which you rated yourself a 4 or 5. Briefly describe what that strategy looks like in your classroom practice. Give a specific example. Think of when you use the strategy; under what conditions; for what instructional goals; why this strategy is the best choice for your students and this lesson. Show, don't tell.

☐ Select one or more strategies that you never or seldom use. Solicit suggestions from other teachers in the group on how you might include this in your practice, and what it looks like in their practice.

☐ What strategy or strategies, not listed above, have you used to help your students achieve? Briefly describe. Share with your colleagues.

☐ Describe how reviewing the effective teaching strategies and your responses makes you feel. Describe why you feel this way.

INSTRUCTIONAL GOALS

Each of the first three portfolio entries asks (not always in these exact words): What were your instructional goals for student learning? *Why are these goals important for these students at this time? How do these goals fit into your overall goals for the year?* The goals you have for your students' learning should be meaningful, important, and relevant beyond the classroom.

Accomplished teachers know and are able to teach the facts, the discreet bits of information associated with the target discipline, but these facts are insufficient as instructional goals. Worthwhile instructional goals address the bigger picture of how these factoids relate to one another and to information outside the specific subject. How do you address the interrelatedness of the world around us? We know, for example, that the cultural and economic dimensions of the rain forest extend beyond its pharmaceutical and biological importance. Literature evolves in an historical context and is enriched when studied from that lens. Historical events take on a different meaning depending on whose point of view we are studying. Students will understand the nature of trees differently if they study them through the lens of a lumberjack, an environmentalist, or a botanist. Important instructional goals guide youngsters in thinking analytically about content and its relevance to the rest of the natural world.

The National Board does not tell you which goals to select or what is worthwhile for your students to know; those decisions are yours. You are expected, however, to analyze why the goals you have selected for your students are important. The instructional goals you feature in your portfolio entries should be large; they should lead students to essential understandings about the world around them. Elaine Johnson in her text *Contextual Teaching and Learning* offers the three scientific principles that underlie nature as ways to organize ideas as they relate to any content area for any grade level. Consider using one of them, or other major themes, as your instructional goal:

1. The principle of interdependence—the interrelatedness of everything, human and nonhuman, with everything else

2. The principle of differentiation—the infinite variety and diversity, the uniqueness of all things in the universe

3. The principle of self-organization—everything is self-ordering, self-maintaining, possessing an interior reality

How you develop any of these themes, or others you select, will be unique to your content area, to the students in your class, to the cultural context of your teaching environment, and to the times in which we live. Completing a textbook chapter, successfully passing a unit exam, or learning how to use a semicolon may not be adequate instructional goals. An instructional goal that leads students to synthesize information from multiple sources may be more valuable than obtaining the information itself.

The portfolio instructions for some of the certificates contain excerpts from the National Content Standards that will help you to choose the big ideas in several content areas addressed in the portfolio.

Considering the rate at which new knowledge is generated and information becomes available (There are more posted Web pages than there are people in the world!), educators need to align instructional goals to the knowledge and skills students will need to be successful within and beyond the classroom.

David Thornburg reports in *The New Basics: Education and the Future of Work in the Telematic Age* that employers are seeking workers who have the following core skills:

1. Digital-age literacy
   ○ Basic scientific, mathematical, and technological literacies
   ○ Visual and information literacies
   ○ Cultural literacy and global awareness
2. Inventive thinking
   ○ Adaptability/ability to manage complexity
   ○ Curiosity, creativity, and risk taking
   ○ Higher-order thinking and sound reasoning
3. Effective communication
   ○ Teaming, collaboration, and interpersonal skills
   ○ Personal and social responsibility
   ○ Interactive communication skills
4. High productivity
   ○ Ability to prioritize, plan, and manage for results
   ○ Effective use of real-world tools
   ○ Ability to create relevant, high-quality products [Thornburg, 59]

Teachers would do well to use any of the above as their instructional goals and then to devise ways for students to demonstrate mastery. Many of these outcomes can best be reached through collaboration with the business community. We'll explore some of the possibilities when we discuss Entry 4: Documented Accomplishments later in the workbook.

Part of the relevance of an instructional goal is its connection to your students at this time. Return to your written Instructional Context piece to reexamine what you wrote about your students. Is there a connection between the two? If not, you could revise what you wrote about the students, and reveal less than you have. Or, and this is what I would hope that you'd do, make certain that what you are electing to teach is relevant for your students.

REFLECTION—ESSENTIAL LEARNING

REFLECTION

Think about your instructional goals, about the big ideas in your discipline(s). Think about the key understandings, the essential learnings you want students to take away from your lesson or unit. Why is it important that students know this information, or understand this idea? How do these big ideas, and your instructional goals, help students prepare for the world beyond the classroom?

ENTRIES 1, 2, AND 3

Entries 1, 2, and 3 are based on student work—for all the certificates. Although there is wide variance between the specific requirements for these three entries, there are more commonalities than there are differences. These entries are about your practice. It doesn't matter if you are a special education teacher working with severely handicapped students or an advanced placement science teacher in a high school for the identified talented and gifted; the overriding concern is about whether or not you add significant value to the students who are in your class. These entries aren't about comparing your practice to someone else's, or moving your students to the level of someone else's students—who may have entered the class at a higher or lower skill level. This is about what you do that makes a difference for your students. And here is why I am so deeply committed to this process. Close the door. Leave the supportive or not supportive administrators outside. Set the mandates aside. It's you and your students. Are they academically enriched because you are their teacher? Accomplished teachers answer with a resounding Yes!

For each of these entries, read the instructions. If you haven't already completed the graphic organizer for backwards-planning the entries, do so. Having an overview is helpful in deciding which students and which lessons you're going to feature. Read the statements that are on the opening pages for each entry. Therein are the guideposts, the benchmarks you'll want to address in your entry. Reread the standards that are highlighted for each entry. If you've already read them once or twice, you'll still benefit from a third read. I've read them dozens of times and I'm still finding key points I missed in the earlier readings. Some of the standards documents are being revised in order to include what we are learning about how we learn. The newly revised standards documents will infuse more technology as well.

All the entries have maximum page allowances. My general rule of thumb is to follow the suggestions to at least within 15 percent. You can't write even a half page more than the maximum number of pages allowed. If you're writing much less than the suggested number of pages, you're probably not being as thorough as you could be. I'm a fairly succinct writer, but I still found myself within a half page of the maximum allowed. The scoring matrix included later in this workbook will be helpful in determining if you've addressed key points for each of the standards.

Every entry provides guiding questions. They all begin with references to the instructional context (discussed earlier in this workbook). There are questions about your school setting, the number and ages of your students, and the relevant characteristics of the class or of the individual student highlighted in your entry that influenced your instructional strategies. Here's where you'll write about the cultural diversity in your class, if there is any, and the variance in ability levels. If you have comments to make about the resources available to you or the room size and configuration, this is where you'll do it. Keep the comments objective, avoid whining. A good rule of thumb is to write out the guiding question and then answer it. If space becomes an issue—if you don't have enough—you can always remove the guiding questions later and condense your responses, but having those guiding questions written out first is an efficient way to make certain you responded to each of them. Know the difference between "maximum pages allowed" and "suggested length." Assessors do not read beyond the maximum page allowance, whereas if you exceed the suggested length for any one section, you'll just have to shorten the following sections.

A more thorough discussion of instructional goals was included earlier in this workbook. Consult the table of contents for the exact location.

It's About the Writing

Yes and no. Writing is a form of communication. Your writing is the main communication between you and the assessors. Although you are not going to lose specific points for misspelled words or grammatical errors, when either gets in the way of the communication, it is going to cost you. There is no one style that wins over any other. Say what you need to say, provide specific examples whenever appropriate, and then get out. Show, don't tell. There is a difference between saying, "I treat all students equally," and describing how you do it: "Each student has a turn at each class job. We use a work-wheel with all the students' names on it. The wheel is rotated daily, or weekly, thus assuring each student has an opportunity to complete each job assignment." The first example tells us that you treat students equitably, but the second example shows us how you do it in ways all assessors can understand. That's what we mean by *Show, don't tell.*

Keep the language simple. There are no bonus points for using education jargon. On the contrary, I find that jargon often gets in the way of clear communication. Besides, some jargon is regional, not national, and the assessor may misunderstand your comments. When in doubt, consult the glossary included with the portfolio instructions and use the definitions you find there when you make word choices to describe your practice.

Direct references to the standards are unnecessary and can get in the way. I've read portfolio entries where the candidate says, "This is in accordance with standard VI, Meaningful Applications of Knowledge." Those references take up valuable space and are a distraction. Besides, the assessors will read beyond your references searching for the evidence of the standard in your practice. This is another case of show, don't tell. If you are addressing the standards in your practice, in the work you assign your students, in how you provide feedback, the assessors will find the standards without you pointing them out.

Likewise, you don't have to make specific references to research you have read, unless your teaching decisions are based on them. Providing a litany of researchers and their pet theories doesn't impress anyone. Stating Vygotsky's Zone of Proximal Development and then teaching way above the students' current ability level doesn't aid your cause. On the other hand, knowing what the students already know, and then pitching your lesson to just a bit above their level—enough to challenge them but not enough to discourage them—is better evidence of accomplished teaching even if you don't know, or don't state, that's Vygotsky's Zone. It is the same as if you describe the context of your teaching and then fail to address the relevant characteristics when you set instructional goals or select strategies to help students reach those goals. Don't go out of your way to quote a theory you don't apply in your practice. However, if it is natural for you to make reference to researchers or theories, then do so, when they are applicable. Be real. Be yourself. This is all about adding value to your student's lives. It is not about razzle-dazzle.

In the 2002–2003 portfolio instructions the National Board gave some examples of descriptive, analytical, and reflective writing. I don't think the examples are very well done, and I do not know if they will change them in subsequent years. The NB does state that the examples given are unscored. Therefore, don't give them an inordinate amount of weight. Your cohort group is more likely to help you to improve your writing, through the questioning techniques, than you'll receive from mimicking styles found in the instructions.

I'm always reluctant to share high-scoring portfolio entries, even my own, with my candidate groups. On the one hand, everyone benefits from seeing some modeling. On the other hand, some candidates think they have to write their entries in the same style as other entries they've read. One way around this is to read only scored portfolio entries in certificate areas other than your own. In that way you can read some examples but you won't be tempted to mimic because the content won't apply.

There are several websites that feature candidate portfolios, chat rooms, and tips. I encourage my candidates to avoid them. Too much of the information is inaccurate or outdated. Sometimes unsuccessful candidates use chat rooms to rant about the unfair assessment practices and bias of the National Board. In 2000 a candidate who didn't achieve certification, but who has published four books, wrote a series of articles about how the National Board scored unfairly. Those of us who have experience with National Board scoring believe that he didn't achieve certification possibly because his entries focused on his achievements rather than those of students. Trust your practice. If you're teaching at an accomplished level, and you communicate that clearly and convincingly, you'll achieve National Board certification.

The certification process is not a test-prep. Just as there isn't one way to teach all students, there isn't one way to successfully complete the portfolio entries. You can, however, follow the instructions, address the standards, and provide *clear, convincing, and consistent* evidence of student accomplishment.

Cream rises to the top, and accomplished teachers achieve certification.

VIDEOTAPING

Two or more of the portfolio entries require accompanying videotapes of your classroom practice. Videotaping should begin early and occur frequently. The more you videotape the more comfortable you and your students will become with a camera in the room. Before beginning to videotape, consult "Getting Started Section 5: Tips for Videotaping," included with your portfolio instructions. There you will find helpful information about equipment, camera placement, and more. In addition to what appears in the instructions, the following comments and ideas will improve instruction and student learning and will also enhance your video entries:

First, remember that the videotape is not about your personal appearance. Dress comfortably and professionally; then don't be critical about your hairstyle, weight, and clothing. (I always suggest to my candidates that they view the first tape at home, alone, with their favorite beverage in hand.) The video is all about your teaching and your interaction with students. It's about how you engage students and how you encourage participation. Your practice videotapes are only that, practice. They will make you more comfortable, help you to improve your practice, and will engage your students in both your National Board process and in their own learning. Students love to be in front of the camera; even shy students sneak a peak when they appear on film.

The more you videotape and analyze what you see and hear, the more likely your teaching will improve. Students benefit also when you ask them to analyze the tapes. You can ask them to describe their behavior, the number and type of questions they ask, how they contribute to the learning environment, and more. Student performances benefit when the rehearsal is taped and analyzed. Seeing and hearing themselves on video has more impact than your evaluation does and may be more instructional than your commentary. In order for anyone to benefit from videotaping, yourself or your students, the classroom environment must be supportive and free from ridicule.

Transcription is powerful. Taking the words from a video is time-consuming but worth it. Having students transcribe their questions and responses and then analyze and reflect upon them generates rich classroom discussion and a great deal of ownership about learning. For the video entry you are submitting with your portfolio, direct quotes taken from your video aid your ability to analyze the lesson.

From my first video I learned how little "wait time" I provided for my students before I answered my own question. I discovered that I preferred the left side of the room to the right, and that some students never got called upon. As a result, I have taught myself to wait for as long as three minutes before asking another question or moving to another student. I make certain my eyes scan the room frequently and I pay more attention to students who are reluctant to respond.

SOAPS—A STRATEGY

Here's another strategy you might find helpful when preparing your written videotape analysis. This is a great strategy to use when analyzing poetry or essays.

S—What is the *subject* of the tape? What big idea do you want the audience to come away with after viewing your videotape? You should be able to state this in a few words. For example: "I want the audience (think assessors) to value the dynamics of the discourse in my class." Or, "In this science lesson I want the assessors to appreciate how student-generated questions guide the laboratory experiment."

O—The *occasion* should be clearly stated in your analysis. What came before the videotaped segment? How did what came before directly lead to what we're seeing in the videotape? Why is this sequence important for these students at this time?

A—Who is the *audience*? This is an easy one to answer. The ultimate audience for this videotape is the assessors scoring your entry. Are you addressing the standards? Does this video follow the instructions? Do you respond to the guiding questions in the written analysis? Have you explained everything that is happening in the video, including the unexpected? The assessor who scores this entry is also a classroom teacher, so you don't need to apologize if one of the students does something that embarrasses you; just explain what happened and how you responded.

P—What is the *purpose* of this videotape and analysis? While the main purpose may be to fulfill the portfolio requirements, take this opportunity to reflect upon and analyze your teaching and your students' learning. You should be able to explain everything the assessor will see in the video, read in the accompanying analysis, and verify through the student artifacts you provide with your entry. Why is the featured lesson important for this group of students at this time? How does this sequence help students to achieve the instructional goals?

S—Who is the *speaker*? The speaker is the voice that tells the story; in this case it's yours. Don't lose your voice. Occasionally I'll read a candidate's entry that is filled with references to researchers; learning theories are featured and the teacher is lost. What is important is that you use your knowledge to inform your instruction. The total entry—video, written analysis and reflection, and student artifacts—should demonstrate with *clear, consistent, and convincing* evidence you have met the NB standards at an accomplished level.

QUALITY VERBAL INTERACTION

In my nine years as a mentor teacher I've had the privilege of observing in many classrooms. I've also viewed more than a hundred videotaped entries. Some classroom practices are dynamic—students are engaged in meaningful ways—and other classrooms lack energy. There is also a marked difference between students simply engaged in an activity (for instance, throwing paper balls into a basket when they spell a word correctly) and students truly focused on learning. Assessors are not looking for lots of activity; they are looking for quality engagement.

Patrick Finn, author of *Literacy With an Attitude*, identifies the level and content of classroom discourse as one of the distinguishing features between domesticating education and liberating, or empowering, education. You can improve the level of your classroom discourse, a key feature of every videotape, by teaching students how to ask questions at every level. Students should be responding not only to the teacher's questions, but to questions posed by other students as well.

Did you know?

- [ ] 85 percent of classroom conversation consists of the teacher asking questions of the students.
- [ ] 85 percent of those questions are "known-response" questions. (The teacher already knows the answer and the student knows the teacher knows.) Students sometimes refer to this kind of questioning as "guessing what's on the teacher's mind."
- [ ] Teachers usually wait an average of less than three seconds between the time they ask a student a question and the time they expect an answer. Learn to wait up to three minutes. Waiting provides a more equal opportunity to respond and to learn for students who are more thoughtful than they are quick.

Transcribing one of your videos will give you a true picture of the discourse activity in your class and the types of questions you ask. To enhance the quality of your classroom discourse, encourage students to ask and answer questions at multiple levels. Level 3 questions, as defined next, are by far the most interesting. Questions should be not only from teacher to student, but between students and from students to teacher. It is often more difficult to frame a question than it is to answer one. Thus asking questions may be the more accurate assessment of a student's understanding than answering, say, a level 1 question.

- [ ] *Level 1 questions* These questions can be answered explicitly by facts contained in the text or by information accessible in other resources. Answers are frequently short, no more than a word or phrase.
- [ ] *Level 2 questions* The answers to these questions are implied in the text. They require analysis and interpretation of specific parts of the text.
- [ ] *Level 3 questions* These questions are more open-ended and go beyond the text. They are intended to provoke a discussion of an abstract idea or issue. These questions often attempt to connect the text, or an idea within the text, to another discipline.

ANALYZING YOUR VIDEOTAPE

The videotape analysis guide that follows is included for you to use as you practice videotaping. If you are working with colleagues, use the analysis guide to critique one another's videos. Remember to use the Looking at Teacher's Work protocol included earlier. Presume good intentions and avoid unproductive harshness. Exposing one's video is personal and involves risk.

VIDEOTAPE ANALYSIS GUIDE

1	**Not at All**
2	**Infrequently or Slightly**
3	**Sometimes or Somewhat**
4	**Often**
5	**Very Frequently or Highly**

For each of the following questions, circle the number to the right that best fits your objective observation of the videotape. Some of the questions may overlap. The purpose is to allow you to get an overall sense of your teaching, or of your colleague's teaching. (These questions have been loosely adapted from the NBPTS instructions.)

OBSERVATION	SCALE				
1. Students talking/asking questions	1	2	3	4	5
2. Student engagement (body language, facial expressions)	1	2	3	4	5
3. Teacher to students—Level 1 questions	1	2	3	4	5
4. Teacher to students—Level 2 questions	1	2	3	4	5
5. Teacher to students—Level 3 questions	1	2	3	4	5

OBSERVATION	SCALE				
	1	2	3	4	5
6. Students to teacher—Level 1 questions	1	2	3	4	5
7. Students to teacher—Level 2 questions	1	2	3	4	5
8. Students to teacher—Level 3 questions	1	2	3	4	5
9. Students' overall interaction with teacher	1	2	3	4	5
10. Students interact with one another	1	2	3	4	5
11. Making connections to students' prior knowledge	1	2	3	4	5
12. Connecting to future learning	1	2	3	4	5
13. Making connections to information/experiences beyond the classroom	1	2	3	4	5
14. Students taking intellectual risks	1	2	3	4	5
15. Putdowns by teacher/other students	1	2	3	4	5
16. Establishing clear learning goals/outcomes	1	2	3	4	5
17. Responding to student misconceptions	1	2	3	4	5
18. Taking advantage of unexpected teachable moments	1	2	3	4	5
19. Differentiated instructional opportunities	1	2	3	4	5
20. Accommodations, if appropriate, for ELD students	1	2	3	4	5
21. Accommodations, if appropriate, for students with special needs	1	2	3	4	5

A strength I observed . . .

An area needing improvement . . .

Suggested ways to improve . . .

I (The teacher) will know I've (he/she has) improved when . . .

ENTRY 4: DOCUMENTED ACCOMPLISHMENTS

Entry 4—Documented Accomplishments is about the work you do beyond your traditional classroom practice that *impacts student learning*. There is little variation between certificates for this entry, so we'll deal with all the certificates at one time. For each accomplishment you describe in this entry, you must also provide some documentation as evidence. In the other entries, you use student work samples as evidence supporting your analysis; in this entry, evidence from outside your classroom is required. Several examples of documents accepted as evidence are clearly explained in the portfolio instructions.

There are three categories addressed in the documented accomplishments entry:

1. *Your life as a learner over the past four years plus the current year of candidacy.* What have you done to consciously and deliberately continue your professional growth? These accomplishments may be as formal as coursework or workshops or as informal as reading a professional book. The key words are consciously and deliberately.

2. *Your work as a leader and professional collaborator over the past four years, plus the current year of candidacy.* This section refers to those activities you engage in with your colleagues and your contributions to the profession. Again, these can be formal connections, as in mentoring or supervising a student teacher, or less formal professional learning networks. Your contributions can be directed to your site colleagues or to the wider education community. Your focus is on improving teaching and learning, not just fulfilling a teacher's basic responsibilities.

3. *Activities to engage your students' families and community in students' learning during the year in which you are working toward Board certification.* Documented accomplishments in this area are those appropriate activities that go beyond what is expected. Meeting with parents at an Open House is usually part of a teacher's responsibility. Documented accomplishment activities go beyond the requirements of the teacher's job; they are interactive, not one-way. The emphasis here is on actively engaging families and communities as teaching and learning partners.

Some of the activities you've been involved in will overlap two or three categories. That's fine. In the past these accomplishments were divided into two portfolio entries. When the Board realized how many activities were overlapping, they combined them into one entry. You still must show accomplishment in each category, but each accomplishment doesn't have to be unique to one category only. Nor do you need to have an equal number of accomplishments from each of the three categories. For instance, if you teach a professional course you are both a professional collaborator contributing to your profession, and you're continuing your own learning—the best way to reinforce learning is to teach. If you have the Junior Achievement program in your class, for example, you are engaging volunteers from the business community as teachers of your students. If some of your families work as volunteers with the Junior Achievement program or some other structured program, you are learning while working collaboratively within the community and engaging family members as teaching and learning partners.

In Entry 4, your task is to describe the activity, analyze its significance, and report its impact on student learning. The assessors are trained to find evidence of the applicable standards wherever they occur in the entry, and that includes within your written analysis, in the concluding reflection, and in the pages of documentation you supply.

Every accomplishment you describe in this entry must be connected to student learning. Therefore, you won't list committee meetings you may have participated in, but that went nowhere. If you read professional journals but can't think of how you related what you read to your classroom practice and to student learning, don't record those activities. Staff development workshops you were mandated to attend, but that didn't improve your teaching, also don't belong in these pages. Likewise, having parents bake cakes for fund-raisers, or attend Open House, is insufficient to demonstrate you engage parents or community members as active teaching and learning partners. Whatever activities you choose to describe for this entry, you must show a connection between the activity and student learning. The students can be in your classes or in the classes of other teachers. The impact can be local, site-specific, or far-reaching.

GUIDED PRACTICE FOR ENTRY 4: DOCUMENTED ACCOMPLISHMENTS

INSTRUCTIONS

1. Read the italicized overview on the first pages of Entry 4 in your certificate's portfolio instructions. Highlight the key ideas, the active verbs. By doing a close read, you'll get some ideas for activities while you're also reminded of activities you've engaged in in the past but might not have considered.

2. Reread the standards that are addressed in this entry. After each entry overview the specific standards to address are listed. Entry 4 usually has only two standards to address. Of course, since all the standards are based on the five core propositions, and since the five core propositions are interrelated, no standard exists in isolation.

3. Enter one or two of your accomplishments on each of the next three pages in the workbook. There may be some overlap; don't worry. Put the activity on the page where it seems to fit best. The purpose here is to make certain that you have some activities in each of the three categories.

4. Talk to other teachers. If you have a cohort group, meet with them to discuss Entry 4. Ask what activities they have done that fit into any of the three designated areas (professional growth, professional collaboration and contribution, outreach to families and community). From this informal survey, enter those activities you've accomplished, but perhaps hadn't thought of until mentioned by another teacher. Note those activities that you may want to incorporate in the future.

5. Before you write up an activity of your own, we'll examine an activity from another portfolio. Then you'll select one activity you have already completed and describe it, include why the activity is significant in your teaching context, and state the impact on student learning.

Note: All the entries in the portfolio require the same type of writing: description, analysis, and reflection. Describe what you did, what it means, why this activity matters to students, and ultimately how this activity or series of activities (think activity in the broadest sense) represents you as an accomplished teacher.

WRITING THE PORTFOLIO ENTRY

☐ *Description:* What did you do? (Activity/What?)

☐ *Analysis:* What does this mean? (Significance/So What?)

☐ *Analysis and Reflection:* Why does this matter? (Impact on student learning/Then what?)

INSTRUCTIONS

☐ In pairs or triads read through the example accomplishment that follows the instructions.

☐ Summarize what the candidate's entry *says*.

☐ What does this activity *mean* to the participants?

☐ Discuss how the entry addresses the applicable standards.

EXAMPLE: TITLE OF ACCOMPLISHMENT— STUDENT-LED CONFERENCES

DESCRIPTION: WHAT IS THE NATURE OF THIS ACCOMPLISHMENT?

Every ten weeks, four times each school year, to coincide with our report cards, I conduct student-led conferences. I first learned about student-led conferences at an English teachers' conference and subsequently read two books on the topic that outlined the theory and the mechanics of putting student-led conferences together. The conferences are in the evening to accommodate my students' families, most of whom are unable to attend daytime meetings and who would otherwise be left out of our school community. I was the first teacher at my school to hold student-led conferences in addition to the required semiannual Open House meetings. Evening meetings are conducted on unpaid time but are very worthwhile nevertheless. Since many of my students live in foster care settings, all adults who play a significant role in the child's life are invited to attend, and do. Students have an opportunity, uninterrupted by me, to explain what they are doing in school and to discuss the progress they are making toward meeting the mandated standards. The students use their portfolios, a collection of the work they have done in class, and the mandated district standards, as the focus of their conference.

ANALYSIS AND REFLECTION: WHY IS THIS ACCOMPLISHMENT SIGNIFICANT?

These conferences are very significant to my students and to their families. Sometimes, they are the only time when students and families have meaningful conversation about schoolwork, when students are able to ask for assistance and be proud of what they have accomplished. I know that the students and families appreciate the time and the structure because by the fourth conference each school year there is nearly 95% participation with several hundred people filling our school cafeteria on a student-led conference evening. They are also significant because most of my students and their families do not have an academic background. Therefore, discourse centered on student work and the standards students are trying to achieve is often absent. Because the conferences begin by following a script, and because the students have done role-playing in our class prior to the first conference, students and their families are more comfortable with the process. Students are also able to conduct the conference in their home language, which also makes families better able to participate.

ANALYSIS AND REFLECTION: HOW HAS WHAT YOU HAVE DESCRIBED HAD AN IMPACT ON STUDENTS' LEARNING?

With student-led conferences, no one hides. Grades are not about what the teacher puts in the roll book, they are about what the student does in school. Students use evidence from their portfolios to document their accomplishments. Because students know early in the school year that there will be an audience for their work, they pay more attention to what they do. I know this is true because even for underperforming students, there is a significant improvement between conferences. Sometimes parents reduce the number of chores they require from older siblings when they understand the impact excessive chores have on their students' schoolwork—a serious issue in a community where children are expected to contribute to the family income or care for younger siblings. Other times parents realize they have been much too lenient and need to monitor their students' work more frequently and cut down on TV watching. By the fourth conference, at the end of the year, nearly all students and their families are in attendance. It's a celebration of student achievement. All in all, everyone wins. One year a parent gave me a copy of the video Mr. Holland's Opus *because of the impact I had on his son. I wish I could say that every student successfully passes from my ninth-grade classes, but that is not so. Most do meet the standards and our tenth-grade teachers always tell me that my students are better prepared than are the students from most of the other teachers.*

Student-led conferences were slow to catch on in my school. It means that what you do in your classroom is now visible to everyone: families, administration, other teachers. The second year two more teachers joined me in doing their own student-led conferences. Now, the administration is encouraging everyone. It hasn't happened yet, but with parents advocating for a change from the traditional Open House to student-led conference nights, it just might go schoolwide.

Documentation included copies of photos of a room full of students and families, a short letter from a parent, and part of a reflection extracted from a student portfolio addressing how these conferences changed his academic life.

DISCUSSION

The preceding activity meets the criteria for a documented accomplishment. It certainly contributed to student learning. It engaged parents as partners in their children's learning by helping them to understand the nature of a portfolio, the district standards, and how they could assist their children academically. There was interaction, not just direction from the teacher to the parents. The candidate continued learning by attending a professional conference and reading books to improve her practice. The candidate impacted her colleagues and the school site as well.

As a side note, this was one of my activities, probably the most effective strategy I ever used. It impacted how I conducted class, instilled reflective practice for my students, engaged the parents, and much more. And it was easy to do, actually making my job as an English Language Arts teacher much less time consuming. For the last six years of my teaching career I held these conferences. With all those hundreds of students I had only one disagreement with a parent about a student's final grade. The students learned that they earned their grades through meeting the standards. What a valuable lesson for them: focused, consistent effort leads to rewards. Now as a teacher of adults I continue to hold my students' portfolios (NB candidates) up to examination by others, and I continue to improve my practice along the way.

Now it's time for you to practice writing one accomplishment for this entry. Your sample doesn't have to meet all three categories, but it might.

☐ Select one of the activities you've listed on the activity pages. Type your response in the required format so you will begin to get a sense of how much you can say on a page. All the entries have maximum page allowances beyond which the assessors will not read.

☐ Description—answer this question: *What is the nature of this accomplishment?* The assessors will know nothing about you except for what they read in your Contextual Information sheet. You must be specific, providing enough detail for the activity to come alive. Keep in mind, however, that you have only a total of twelve pages in which to document all your accomplishments. During the drafting stages don't worry about the length. You'll have time to select the most meaningful accomplishments and to revise your writing later.

☐ Analysis and reflection: *Why is this accomplishment significant?* Your accomplishment doesn't have to be original; mine wasn't. It does have to be effective and have significance in your teaching context. To do this well, you need to understand your context (Completing the Contextual Information sheet is helpful in informing you, as well as the assessor, about your context.) and construct activities that address the challenges of your teaching environment. It is nearly impossible to completely separate analysis from reflection. When we think about what the activity means it is intricately connected to why it matters.

☐ More analysis and reflection: *How has what you have described had an impact on students' learning?* You don't have to provide test scores, you can use anecdotal commentary. The documentation you provide as evidence should directly relate to what you have described. Direct quotes are always powerful.

☐ With your cohort group, using the Reflective Conversation Questions and the Looking at Teachers' Work protocol, if you find them helpful, critique and comment on one another's drafts.

Remember that the candidate has written about only one activity, and will write about many more, prior to completing Entry 4. Therefore, don't expect one activity to meet the criteria of *clear, consistent, and convincing* evidence of having met the standards. The assessors score the entry in its entirety.

There is no set number of activities that will assure accomplishment for this entry category. I have read entries describing two dozen activities, and others with only eight. What's important is that you have made an impact; that you continue to grow and learn; that you understand the importance of opening your practice to families and the greater community.

When you have completed your initial descriptions and analysis of the activities for this entry, you'll then write a two-page reflective summary that examines the patterns you see emerging. Most candidates have never stepped back and examined their practice in this way. You can't write the reflection until you've drafted the entire entry. It is only as you prepare your reflection that you'll be able to make final choices, cutting those activities of least impact, or that were isolated events that may have impacted your students, but didn't leave an impression on you.

In my portfolio, after reviewing the activities I described in preparation for writing the reflective summary, I recognized two major themes. The first was that I stressed personal responsibility—for teachers, for parents, and most definitely for students. Student-led conferences, for example, were about students acknowledging that their work was the basis for their grades, not the teacher's subjective reaction. The second theme that emerged was my wide-ranging involvement in professional development, my own and that of my colleagues. It was these themes that have continued to guide my career. I now work full-time in the field of professional development. All this work really took focus during my year of National Board candidacy. The process is powerful.

DOCUMENTED ACCOMPLISHMENTS—SOME SUGGESTIONS

I have found that many of my colleagues, especially those who teach in secondary school, have little experience working with families or community members as teaching and learning partners. That was certainly the case for me when I became a National Board candidate. It has since become one of my strongest areas and has greatly impacted my students' learning. Here are some outreach suggestions:

☐ Junior Achievement is a nonprofit, community-based organization that began more than eight decades ago. Its mission is to help students learn about our free-enterprise system. It does this through a K–12 curriculum, aligned with state and district content standards. Junior Achievement–trained volunteers from the business community come to your school over a period of time, usually four to eight weeks, and for one period each week they teach age-appropriate facets of our free-enterprise system. There is no cost to the teacher, school, or district. Junior Achievement trains the volunteers and provides the curriculum and all necessary supplies. For more information, and to find the Junior Achievement office in your area, consult the website: *www.ja.org.*

☐ Other community-based organizations undoubtedly could easily be tapped into. I've recently begun to work with our area Rotary Club whose members have developed an Adopt-A-School program working with one of our local school districts. The goal is to work with community members as teaching and learning partners.

☐ Service learning, as opposed to community service, matches community needs to the curriculum. Students research their community, identify a need, and then develop a service project to meet that need. Teachers coordinate the curriculum to enrich the experience. For instance, a food drive becomes a service learning project when a food bank is asked what food they need. Students learn about nutrition and serving sizes, develop menus, and canvas the community for food stuffs specific to the menus they've developed. There are opportunities in this project for developing skills in math, writing, telephone communication, nutrition and health, and much more. Students who reach out to help others benefit academically and socially. Consult the Internet for more examples of Service Learning projects.

☐ Service Learning projects provide opportunities for the NB candidate to continue personal learning, work with colleagues across grade levels and disciplines, and engage family and community members in student learning. You cover all three Entry 4 categories with this one.

☐ Student-led conferences have had the greatest impact on my students' learning and my teaching of any strategy I've ever used. Students share their portfolios, evidence of their efforts to meet the designated content standards, with their families and other community members. There are several excellent books on the topic and lots of free information on the Internet. I'm convinced that the description of my student-led conferences, and the accompanying documentation, contributed to my high score on Entry 4.

ASSESSMENT CENTER EXERCISES

In addition to the four portfolio entries, each candidate must complete six assessment center exams of thirty minutes each. Unless the candidate makes arrangements for special accommodations, all these exams are done on the same day at one of hundreds of computer testing centers located around the country. The candidate has a six-month window in which to schedule an appointment and take the exams. The exams may not be scheduled, however, until after all the $2,300 in fees have been paid. Once candidates have taken the exams, even if they have not yet submitted their portfolio, the NB fees are nonrefundable.

I strongly suggest, as do many of my colleagues who support candidates, that you complete your portfolio entries before taking the assessment exams. Most candidates feel more confident writing about student learning and their own teaching after they have spent several months on their portfolio entries.

Unlike the portfolio entries, which have many commonalities, the assessments are certificate-specific, stressing content knowledge. Some exams require candidates to analyze student work samples and suggest next-steps for student achievement. Others test for deeper levels of knowledge in specific disciplines. The National Board website includes information about the assessments. There you will find the exam categories for your certificate. Most of the assessments must be completed electronically. There is some accommodation for math symbols. The exams are usually written, but are aural for world language and music. Consult the website for task-specific information.

Candidates have reported that their typing skills impacted their test results. You have only thirty minutes for each exam. If you are still a two-finger typist, you will be at a disadvantage. Practice, practice, practice keyboarding. Here's another reason for submitting the portfolio first: you'll have spent months typing and will most likely have improved.

Do complete the online tutorial in order to become better acquainted with the computer directions. You want this experience to be about teaching, not about computer skills, or lack thereof.

Some candidates have test phobia. If you fall into this category, practice by taking a timed test. Ask members of your cohort group to write test prompts to share, and then duplicate test conditions. I have found this greatly reduces test anxiety.

Together the six exams are worth only 40 percent of the total NB score. If you do not achieve certification on the first attempt, you can elect to redo any of the exams on which you have scored poorly. You will not have to redo all the exams, unless you choose to.

Relax. If you know your content area, if you've spent months analyzing your student work, you'll be fine. They're just tests; your students take tests all the time and they manage; you can also.

SCORING

Standards-based instruction begins with the standards against which the student or, in the case of the National Board, the candidate will be assessed. The standards are followed by clear instructions for demonstrating accomplishment, and a scoring guide by which the student's performance, or candidate's entry, will be scored. National Board certification is standards-based performance assessment of the highest caliber. Nothing is hidden, nothing is left to chance. Everyone knows up front what is expected and how to meet those expectations.

Classroom teachers should provide this same structure for students: the standards to be addressed; clear, explicit instructions; and a scoring guide by which the student's efforts will be measured. The National Board uses a four-point scoring guide. The actual points aren't what is important. What is important is that you, or the student, know in advance what is expected, so you can accurately assess your own work.

For each entry, the National Board includes a section "How Will My Response Be Scored?" The following is taken verbatim from the portfolio instructions for MC/GEN, Entry 1. Although the details vary from certificate to certificate, and from entry to entry within each certificate, all entries contain a Level 4 rubric. This one is representative of all the scoring guides.

The Level 4 rubric, the highest level of achievement, specifically requires *clear, consistent, and convincing* evidence in your response that you:

- [ ] Identify high, worthwhile, and appropriate goals for student learning and set appropriate objectives to meet those goals
- [ ] Engage students in meaningful exploration of ideas through the use of writing [specific for this entry's requirements]
- [ ] Use varied assignments to build student understanding and writing skills
- [ ] Describe, analyze, and evaluate student work and classroom instruction with insight about students and their learning
- [ ] Engage in reflective thinking that demonstrates a clear understanding of past teaching and constructive ideas for future teaching

☐ Plan tasks that enable students to use writing as a tool for learning, as a way of acquiring and organizing new information, and as a means of enjoyment

Use the Level 4 rubric provided with each entry to plan your entry. Use it again when you're writing your responses to the guiding questions. And refer to it still a third time when you have completed your draft and you're self-scoring, or scoring with your cohort group.

For the first several years I worked with National Board portfolios I completely missed their careful choice of the word response. In my mind response was interchangeable with answer. This was a mindful choice on behalf of the National Board. Answers tend to be specific and limited. Responses are open-ended and filled with possibilities. How you respond to each of the entries is open-ended and filled with possibilities.

HOW SCORING AND CERTIFICATION WORK

Each performance, portfolio entry, or assessment center exam is scored independently on a 0.75 to 4.25 score scale.

THE SCORE SCALE

0.75 1.00 1.25	1.75 2.00 2.25	2.75 3.00 3.25	3.75 4.00 4.25
The "1" Family	The "2" Family	The "3" Family	The "4" Family

The score scale is a modified four-point score scale. Performances are assigned a whole number score (1, 2, 3, or 4) and then, if appropriate, the whole number score is augmented with a plus or minus. Plus and minus scores are represented numerically as an increment or decrement of 0.25 from the whole number score. For example, a 1+ is equivalent to a 1.25, a 3– is equivalent to a 2.75. Scores can range from 0.75 to 4.25.

Assessors classify performances into the score category that best fits the performance, and then they may "shade" the score up or down to reflect a strong or weak performance in that category. Families are distinct from one another; cases must ultimately be assigned to one family or another, not in between.

To achieve certification the candidate must accumulate 275 points out of a possible 400 (actually, it's possible to score 425). Portfolio entries and assessment exercises are weighted. Entries 1, 2, and 3 are each worth 16 percent of the total score. Entry 4, documented accomplishments, is worth 12%. Each assessment center exam is worth 6.67 percent. The total portfolio counts for 60 percent of the final grade, the assessment center only 40 percent. Put your effort where you'll get the greatest payoff. Scores are cumulative. It is possible to receive a low score on one entry or one test but still achieve certification because another entry or test scored high.

Candidates who do not achieve certification at the first attempt (Notice I don't use the words pass or fail because everyone who completes is a winner; actually, everyone who attempts is a winner.) may bank their scores for twenty-four months. Candidates then determine which entries or exams they want to retake. If you retake a portfolio entry, it is the same one you did before, only with your current students. If you elect to redo an assessment center exam, you will have a new exam in the same category as the one you took originally, but not the same exact prompt. The score from a retake entry or exam automatically replaces the original score, even if it is lower. About half of all candidates who don't achieve at the first attempt, do achieve at the second attempt. Few candidates drop out of the process.

BIAS IN SCORING

Forget bias in scoring, there isn't any. This is the most thoughtful, the fairest scoring process, I have ever been associated with and I've scored state exams, Disney teacher awards, the Skirball National Essay contest, and more. Assessors are classroom teachers in your certificate area. They receive four days of intensive training to rid themselves of any personal biases that may affect scoring. They study the standards, and then they study the standards again. They calibrate the entry they will be scoring and score the same entry for an entire three-week period. They read so thoroughly, they can usually score only about eight candidates' entries a day. This is a time-consuming, expensive assessment process and that's how your NB fees are spent. Although the National Board has a method whereby you can contest your score, I don't know anyone who has successfully done so. I have, however, worked with a number of banking candidates who upon careful, and objective, rereading of their entries, felt they could have written more thoroughly or more clearly about their classroom practice and did so on their retake entry.

Portfolio Scoring Matrix

Certificate: _____

Directions: In the left column enter the title of each of the standards for your certificate. In each of the next four columns, mark an X for each standard you are to address in the entry. Using a different color, read your response to each entry and mark an X each time you find evidence of the standard. You're accomplished if you find clear, consistent, and convincing evidence in your response for each required standard.

Standard	Entry 1:	Entry 2:	Entry 3:	Entry 4:
I.				
II.				
III.				
IV.				
V.				
VI.				
VII.				
VIII.				
IX.				
X.				
XI.				
XII.				
XIII.				
XIV.				
XV.				

Scoring Your entry—Take 2

Directions: In the left column enter the key points for each of the standards that apply to this entry. You'll need to make several copies of this page. Carefully read your portfolio entry response. Mark with an X each time you find evidence you have addressed this standard. Record the nature of the evidence. We're looking for *clear, consistent, and convincing* evidence. For an even more accurate assessment, ask members of your cohort group to score your portfolio entry. If they find the evidence, there is a good chance the assessor will also. If they don't find clear, consistent, and convincing evidence, consider revising your entry.

Standard— Key Points	Evidence (Be specific. Show, don't tell.):					

REFERENCES

Bransford, J. D., Brown, A. L., et al., Eds. (2000). *How People Learn.* Washington D.C., National Academy Press.

Finn, P. J. (1999). *Literacy With an Attitude.* Albany, State University of New York Press.

Johnson, E. B. (2002). *Contextual Teaching and Learning.* Thousand Oaks, Corwin Press, Inc.

Thornburg, D. (2002). *The New Basics: Education and the Future of Work in the Telematic Age.* Alexandria, Association for Supervision and Curriculum Development.

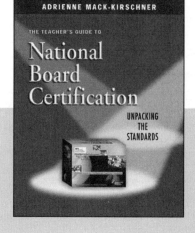
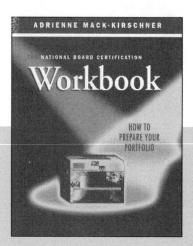